GREEN TREASURE

By Joy Cowley

Illustrated by E. Silas Smith

DOMINIE PRESS

Pearson Learning Group

Paperback ISBN 0-7685-1091-0
Printed in Singapore
12 13 VOZF 14 13 12 11

Dominie Press
Pearson Learning Group

1-800-321-3106
www.pearsonlearning.com

Table of Contents

Chapter One
A Mystery Mission

"It's a special mission," Conrad's mother said. "We're going to Xedor 2, but I can't tell you why until we get there."

Conrad was almost crazy with curiosity. His mom, Captain Edna, commanded an ore wagon that carried freight to Mars. Then one day, there were highly secret meetings with important Martian leaders. Captain Edna, Conrad, and her crew were flown away to a hidden launching site on the great Martian plain. There, they boarded a small, new ship with a full science lab on board.

Conrad knew the ship belonged to the Mars Research Institute, but there were no familiar markings on the outside. In fact, there were no markings at all.

"It must be a pirate ship!" he joked.

His mother didn't laugh. "That's enough, Conrad!" she said.

The rest of the crew were tight-lipped. Mr. Jefferson the engineer, Officer Zeej, Officer Ching, even Dr. Vakalau, who was in charge of the laboratory—none of them would say a word about the mission. Conrad had to work it out for himself.

He made notes on his homework computer.

1. My mother is a flight commander and a geologist. She knows a lot about ships and rocks.

2. This ship has got such a big science lab, there's no space for a games room.

3. The mission to Xedor 2 must be about some new kind of mineral.

4. There is so much secrecy, this mineral must be very valuable or very dangerous. Maybe both.

He tapped a few keys to look in the Intergalactic Atlas and find out more about Xedor 2. A misty brown ball came up on his screen. Xedor 2 was one of twin satellites of the planet Demeter. It was small, and all of its water was frozen. The atmosphere was similar to that on Mars. The air could not support known life.

Conrad sighed. There was no mention of any important minerals.

Chapter Two
Landing Party

Tweet, the ship's computer, had a soft, singing voice. "Prepare for a primitive landing," it crooned.

Conrad knew that *primitive* meant *rough*. There were no landing stations on Xedor 2. They had to land among rocks or maybe even quicksand. If the ship was damaged, they'd never be able to take off again.

But the landing was surprisingly simple. A shudder went through the vessel as it went into reverse thrust, then there was a little bump. A puff of brown dust rose around them and slowly settled. All over the bridge there was a click of buckles as the crew undid their harnesses.

"Landing party prepare to disembark," said Captain Edna, who was now at the computer. "Tweet, how much time do we have?"

"Five hours until Xedor 2 nightfall," Tweet replied.

"That'll be fine," said Dr. Vakalau. "We're near the site. It won't take us long to collect the samples."

"So it *is* about minerals," Conrad thought as he jumped down from his seat. He followed Officer Ching to get his space suit, but his mother called him back.

"No, Conrad. We stay here," she said.

He turned to look at her. She had spoken not in her *mom* voice, but in her *captain* voice, and he didn't dare argue. He made a face. This was probably the only chance he'd ever have to walk on the satellite Xedor 2.

"Is it dangerous?" he asked.

"No more dangerous than Mars," said his mother. "Dr. Vakalau has been here several times. But this is a special mission, Conrad. You don't have clearance to go out there."

"Who can give me clearance?" he asked. "Dr. Vakalau?"

Captain Edna sighed. "Conrad, I admire your spirit of adventure. But please, don't make this difficult for me. I have my orders."

A little voice inside him wanted to say, *what orders?* The voice wanted to whine and yell: *it's not fair!* He swallowed and looked at the surface of Xedor 2 through Tweet's computer screen. It was a boring place, he told himself, another

blob of lifeless rock floating in the universe. There was no reason why anyone would want to go there.

The screen flickered and changed to four suited figures standing beside the ship's airlock. Conrad moved closer to look at their face plates—Zeej, Ching, Jefferson, Vakalau. But why were they carrying those round duro-glass cases?

"Landing party ready to exit ship," sang Tweet.

"Release doors," said Captain Edna.

Conrad watched the landing procedure. Several times, he had been with a landing party collecting mineral samples. Rocks were placed in wire baskets. Dust went into metal tubes.

He said to his mother, "What kind of rock has to go into a duro-glass case?"

His mother, who was watching the screen, didn't answer.

"Mom?" he insisted. "Why do they have duro-glass cases?"

She ran her hand through her short, fair hair. "Conrad," she said, "they're not collecting rocks."

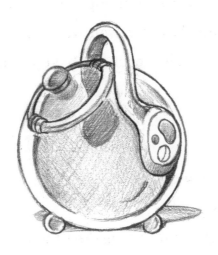

Chapter Three

For the Good of the Planet

The laboratory looked new. It was a place of metal and plastic, shining under a hard white light. Against the far wall was a row of empty duro-glass cases, each with separate climate controls.

"These are for plants," Captain Edna told Conrad.

"Living plants?" he asked.

She nodded.

"I thought that was against the law," he said. "I thought you couldn't take a living organism from one world to another."

His mother rested her hand on one of the cases. She said, "Conrad, Xedor 2 is a lot like Mars. What is our biggest problem on Mars?"

"Lack of oxygen," he replied.

"Yes. Air we can breathe. Now imagine, Conrad, if we had a life-supporting atmosphere on Mars. We wouldn't have to live in atmospheric domes. We wouldn't have the problem of having to produce oxygen. Can you imagine walking out of a Martian dome without a space suit?"

He shook his head.

"One day that will happen," she said. "It's only a matter of time. Dr. Vakalau thinks the hope for Mars is here on Xedor 2. He has discovered a new form of plant life. It's an organism that moves across the land. It feeds on the iron salts in the soil, and it releases large amounts of oxygen into the atmosphere."

"So we're going to take these plants back to Mars," he said.

"Dr. Vakalau calls them *grenoxes*. He says that in a few years there'll be grenox farms all over the planet. They'll release the oxygen we need. As the atmosphere changes, other life forms will grow. It's very exciting, Conrad. But you can't mention this to any of your friends."

"Because it's not legal," he said.

His mother frowned. "According to Intergalactic Code, it's not strictly legal. But the Martian Government has put a lot of thought into this project. Everyone realizes there are times when the law can be bent."

"So Dr. Vakalau really *is* a pirate," said Conrad.

"Nonsense!" snapped his mother. "Dr. Vakalau is a great man. What he's doing is for the good of our planet and its people. Believe me, what he's doing is right."

Conrad was silent. He remembered all the stories his mother had told him about Earth and how the atmosphere had been poisoned by people who were sure they were right. He followed his mother back to the bridge in time to hear Tweet say, "Mission completed."

Conrad looked through one of the windows and saw a truck with dozens of duro-glass cases on it.

Tweet sang, "Landing party ready to board with samples."

Chapter Four
Headaches

Conrad thought the only thing that could love a grenox was another grenox. They were very ugly, nothing like the plastic models of Earth plants he'd seen in the museum. Each grenox was bigger than his hand, bright green, and scaly. Their shapes varied, but basically there was a thick stem on a flat base. The base rippled when a plant moved over its glass cage.

"We've got both male and female plants," said Dr. Vakalau, putting a gloved hand into the cage. "This is a fine male specimen." The instant he touched the grenox, it stopped moving. It shrunk, pulling in its stem and the floppy part of its base. What lay in Dr. Vakalau's hand now looked like a large blob of green putty covered in scales.

"It's interesting the way they do that," said Officer Ching, as she, too, picked up a grenox. "It's a survival skill. That means Xedor 2 could have other life forms that threaten grenoxes."

"Not life forms," said Dr. Vakalau. "Storms. This is how they protect themselves from the fierce ice storms that batter them. Watch this." He threw the blob of green putty across the lab. It hit the far wall with a loud clang and fell to the floor with another clang. "See how strong they are?"

"Please, no!" said Officer Zeej, holding his head. "I have a headache."

"We've all got headaches," muttered Mr.

Jefferson. "Do you think our oxygen packs were contaminated?"

Dr. Vakalau picked up the grenox. "The last time I was here, I had a headache, but it passed. I believe the dense gravity of this satellite causes a change in blood pressure. We were probably out there too long."

Conrad's mother put her hand on her head. "My head hurts, and I haven't been out of the ship." She turned to Conrad, a question in her eyes.

"No," said Conrad. "I'm okay. No headache."

"The pain will disappear when we leave this place," Dr. Vakalau said. He took the other grenox from Officer Ching and put them both back in their glass cases. They lay blob-like on a bed of reddish-brown gravel.

Captain Edna rubbed her forehead. "Secure

the lab and then come up to the bridge. We'll need to move. In half an hour there'll be darkness and the possibility of an ice storm."

Dr. Vakalau adjusted the climate control on the glass case. He was smiling in spite of his headache. "This is a great moment," he said. "We finally have our cargo of green treasure. Believe me, it will be the greatest treasure in the history of Mars."

Chapter Five

The Only Sign of Life

They had traveled more than a day from Xedor 2, and the headaches had become worse. Officer Ching had to go to her bunk. The rest of the crew worked slowly, their faces pale, with dark marks under their eyes.

Conrad was the only one who wasn't in pain. "Can I go into the lab?" he asked Dr. Vakalau.

"Yes, yes. Five minutes only." Dr. Vakalau had a nosebleed, which he was mopping with tissues. "Don't touch anything," he added.

Conrad stood by the grenoxes, hoping that one would move. Nothing happened. They were all at the bottom of their glass cases, lying still in their blob form. The only sign of life was a faint pulsing under the green scales.

Conrad felt sorry for the plants. He was sure they felt threatened. "You'll like Mars." He tried to sound cheerful. "It's much bigger than Xedor 2."

"Ah!" Dr. Vakalau came in. "So you are talking to our green treasure. Aren't they beautiful? Thirty-six fine grenoxes!"

"They don't look very happy," Conrad said.

"Give them a day or two and they'll adjust." Dr. Vakalau mopped at his bleeding nose. "You're a scientist aren't you? Then you can stay and watch. I'm going to dissect a grenox."

"You're going to *what*?" cried Conrad.

"Blast this headache!" Dr. Vakalau put his hand to his brow. "I'm going to cut a grenox into thin slices for tissue culture. I'm going to clone these plants." He put his hand into a case and brought out one of the green, scaly blobs. "If we have to wait for them to breed naturally, the project will take years. Ah, but if we use cloning, within months we should have millions of grenoxes, all releasing oxygen into the Martian atmosphere. Think of it!"

The grenox quivered slightly as Dr. Vakalau put it on the steel bench and picked up a knife. Conrad stepped backward. He couldn't watch this.

"Ya-a-a-ah!" screamed Dr. Vakalau, dropping his knife and clutching his head. "No, oh no! It hurts!" He took two steps toward Conrad, then his knees bent and he fell to the floor.

Conrad stared, open-mouthed. He ran to Dr. Valakau, then looked up at the grenox.

He stepped over Dr. Vakalau, picked the grenox up from the bench, and gently put it back in its case.

Then he pushed the alarm button for help.

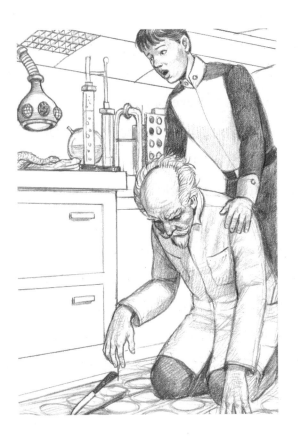

Chapter Six

Racing Gray Lines

Dr. Vakalau and Officer Ching were unconscious in their bunks. Mr. Jefferson's headache was so bad that he couldn't move out of his chair. His nose, too, was bleeding. Conrad's mother looked as though she hadn't slept for months.

"It's the plants, isn't it?" Conrad said. "They're causing the headaches."

"We think so," she said. "They could be releasing some poison that's making us ill. Are you sure you haven't got a headache?"

"Absolutely sure," he replied. "I feel fine."

"I'm glad to hear it," she said. "But I don't

know why you're not affected." She turned her pain-filled eyes to Officer Zeej, who was coming through the door. "Did you get it?" she asked.

Officer Zeej slowly nodded and held up a disk. "I also gave them sedatives to calm the wild brain activity."

Captain Edna explained to Conrad, "Officer Zeej has done brain scans of Officer Ching and Dr. Vakalau. We're hoping Tweet can tell us what's causing the headaches."

Officer Zeej fed the disk to Tweet and pressed some keys. The large screen filled with racing gray lines.

"This means nothing," said Officer Zeej.

"Tweet," said Captain Edna, "tell us what's on this disk."

Tweet's voice, normally musical, became a high-pitched shriek. Conrad put his hands over his ears, and his mother hurried to turn down the volume. The screaming dropped to a shrill hum with regular whistling noises. The racing gray lines jumped up and down like little snakes.

Officer Zeej said, "The only person who might understand this is Dr. Vakalau, and he is beyond understanding anything."

Conrad watched and listened. There were patterns in the gray lines, patterns in the shrill humming. "I know this sounds ridiculous," he said, "but do you think this could be some kind of language?"

"You're right," said Officer Zeej. "That *is* ridiculous. This is a brain scan. You're looking at the electrical impulses of Dr. Vakalau's brain. They are far from normal, but this isn't any language I've ever seen."

Conrad's mother stared more closely at the screen. "Language?" she repeated.

"Yes," Conrad said. "Plant language."

His mother glanced at him and then spoke to the computer. "Tweet, does this disk contain a form of communication?"

"Affirmative," replied Tweet in its normal sing-song voice. "There are repetitive signals containing ordered information and instructions."

"Can you translate it for us?" she asked.

For a few seconds, a soft whirring sound replaced the shrill hum. Then Tweet's voice came back. "Negative. This form of communication is beyond my programming."

There was a tense silence, while Conrad's mother tried to think of something else to try.

Then Tweet said, in its sweet voice, "There is a similar module that is in the library, but it is not in my database. Insert the cartridge for program KL303: *Extraordinary Vibrations*."

"Extraordinary Vibrations," said Conrad's mother, looking through the disk files. "Here it is." She took out a small crystal cartridge and inserted it into the computer.

The gray lines continued to dance on the screen. Tweet sang, "Accessing. Learning. Processing."

About a minute later, instead of the high-pitched whining sound, Tweet started speaking in slow, broken tones.

"Please," it sang, "will you... return us... for there is... no life, no good for us... in this place. Why do you... take us away... when we are... not in wrong-doing? Please... alien life form... return us... for there is no life, no good for us in this place."

"That must be what's been causing our headaches!" cried Conrad's mother. "Their voices in our minds! They've been trying to talk to us, but we aren't equipped to receive their language."

"Why did you take us away... when we are not wrong-doing?" sang Tweet. "Please, oh alien life form..."

"They're not just plants," said Conrad. "They're intelligent beings!"

His mother sighed and rubbed her head. "Who says plants are not intelligent?" she replied. "The whole universe is intelligent. This is a mistake! I have to correct it."

"You're going back to Xedor 2?" Conrad asked.

She didn't answer because she was already giving an order to the computer.

"Tweet, please tell the life forms in the laboratory that we are sorry. We will return them. In approximately 14 hours they will be home. Oh, and Tweet? Please ask them to cease their communication with us."

"With pleasure, Captain Edna," Tweet replied.

"Wait!" cried Officer Zeej. "Captain, this will finish Dr. Vakalau's plans to bring oxygen to Mars. It will mean that our mission is a failure."

"A mission is not a failure if you learn something from it," said Captain Edna. "I've learned that no project is so important that we need to take slaves. Right, Zeej? Now, let's turn this ship around."

Conrad wanted to hug his mother, but instead he smiled and stepped out of her way. "Why didn't I get the headache?" he asked.

The answer came not from his mother, but from the computer. "The captives you call grenoxes attempted to communicate with the mature aliens," sang Tweet. "They did not attempt to communicate with the immature alien."

Conrad's mother laughed. "They thought you were just a kid," she said. "Hey! You know something? My headache's gone."

"Mine, too," said Officer Zeej.

Conrad left the bridge. He ran to the laboratory and turned on the lights. The grenoxes were no longer unmoving blobs. They were rippling over the glass, their stems waving like soft green fingers.

"Wow!" Conrad said.

Almost immediately, there was a sharp pain in his head. It began above his eyes and spread to the back of his hairline. His eyes watered with pain, but he didn't mind. He bowed toward the glass cases. "Thanks to you, too," he said.